Guido Biagi

The private Life of the Renaissance Florentines

Guido Biagi

The private Life of the Renaissance Florentines

ISBN/EAN: 9783337110796

Printed in Europe, USA, Canada, Australia, Japan

Cover: Foto ©ninafisch / pixelio.de

More available books at **www.hansebooks.com**

THE PRIVATE LIFE OF THE RENAISSANCE FLORENTINES ▲ BY DR GUIDO BIAGI ▲

With 30 illustrations.

FLORENCE, 1896
R. BEMPORAD & SON
PUBLISHERS

Reprinted by kind permission from Blackwood's Magazine, *March 1893*

All rights reserved

303-96. - Printed by S. LANDI - Florence

THE PRIVATE LIFE
OF THE
RENAISSANCE FLORENTINES

It is not easy to form an idea of what the city of Florence was like in the fourteenth and fifteenth centuries. To those who look down on her from one of the heights that form so beautiful a crown around her ramparts, and which to-day are covered with innumerable gardens gay with flowers, but which then were dark with densely foliaged trees, bushes, and jungles, she would have appeared a gloomy mass of battlemented towers, encompassed by walls and bulwarks.

The public buildings that we admire today, the graceful cupolas of the churches, the bell-

The Marzocco.

towers whose voices repeat the heart-beats of a
nation, did not yet stand out against a back-

Or San Michele. Shrine by *Orcagna.*

ground of deep-blue sky like the huge masts of
a mighty vessel. The third cincture of walls that
enclosed the city, whose demolition our own
day has witnessed, was not yet completed, and

Arno made a bend near the Piazza di Santa Croce, issuing from the Ponte a Rubaconte and

Santa Reparata, and the Campanile.
(From a Laurentian Ms.).

the Castle of Altafronte. This was in the early times of the fourteenth century, when the little Church of Santa Reparata was still extant, and the very name of Santa Maria del Fiore was unknown. In the place where later stood the *loggia* of Or San Michele the corn-market was held; the tower begun by Giotto, and called after his name, had not yet been carried up to the last tier of windows by Francesco Talenti; only

The *Baptistery*. (Miniature in the *Biadajolo*, a Laurentian Ms.).

on the tower of the Palazzo dei Priori the great bell of the people, known as the *vacca,* already bellowed forth its deep brazen tones, evoking the echoes of the sweet voice of liberty.

The Cornchandler. (Miniature in the *Biadajolo*).

The miniatures of the " Biadajolo " the frescoes of the Bigallo, barely give a notion of the Florence of those days. They are rather fanciful representations made at a period when perspective was stil unknown, and the brilliant red roofs con-

Santa Reparata and the *Campanile*. (Miniature in the *Biadajolo*).

trast too vividy in tone with the forest of towers that intertwine and seem to mount one on the top of other. The painting by Domenico di Michelino that can still be seen in the Duomo endeavours to show the Florence of Dante, whose figure is a conspicuous object in the very centre of the

Loggia del Bigallo by *Orcagna*.

picture; but this also is a fancy Florence, imaginary like the " Purgatorio " and " Inferno " which the artist has painted close beside it. A more recent view of the city can be seen in the " Assumption of the Virgin " by Botticelli, painted for Matteo Palmieri, and now in the English National Gallery. The subject was taken from Palmieri's poem " La città di Vita, " and the painting was at the time considered almost heretical, because the artist had depicted the Virgin as received into the glory of heaven, surrounded by a sublime vision of female angels. But the landscape that serves as a background to this marvellous composition is so lost in the distance and in the shadows of a golden twilight, that it does not help us much in our quest. It is only later on that our desire is gratified, when we

A plan of Florence. (*Chronicles of Nüremberg*).

can see a plan of the city as it appeared at the end of the fifteenth century in the "Chronicles of Nüremberg."

But in order faithfully to picture Florence from the thirteenth century to the glorious days of the

Renaissance, when the treasures that her merchants had garnered from all parts of the world were poured forth for the creation of immortal monuments, following up the traditions of art inaugurated by Arnolfo, Giotto, and Orcagna,—to picture these scenes, which should be peopled with figures of artisans, merchants, women, friars, monks, jugglers, hawkers, poets, story-tellers, men-at-arms, rustics, pages, knights, that crowd the canvas—to give an even incomplete idea of the history of the Florentine people, that from medieval manners upraised themselves to the polish of the Renaissance,—to do this would be the work of an artist who was at the same time an archæologist and a poet. Nor would this suffice. But until this artist arise, if ever it be possible, who shall thus teach us by sight, we must content ourselves with tasting only such palatable bits as can be extracted from old books of reminiscences, domestic chronicles, and private correspondence, from story-tellers and poets, from dusty archives and forgotten records. Here embedded are many interesting particulars, many anecdotes, many items of news that help to give an insight into the life of that time, so remote even from our imagination.

In the narrow crowded streets, beside the massive stone palaces secure as fortresses, with their embattled towers rising proudly above their heads, crouched roofs and windows covered with oiled linen in lieu of glass. These houses were always exposed to danger by fire, wherefore Paolo di Ser Pace da Certaldo, a writer of the fourteenth century, whose interesting record lies unpublished in the Riccardiana Library, counselled that the people should always keep ready twelve large sacks, " in which to put your things whenever there is fire in your vicinity or anywhere even near to you or in your house, and also thick cord to reach from the roof to the ground, so as to enable you to escape from the window." The dusty streets were never swept, except by the water that ran like a rivulet in and out of the gutters, in which, as Sacchetti tells us in his famous " novels, " those animals specially protected by Sant'Antonio used to grubble, " after which they will pay visits in the neighbouring houses, bringing with them dirt, confusion, and disorder." Not that these houses were patterns of cleanliness. They were swept once a week, on Saturdays; on other days the refuse was tossed under the bed, where could be found a little of everything, such as fruit-parings, cores, bones, plucked chickens, and live fowls, cackling geese, and an abundance of cobwebs. These were just the modest dwellings of a people satisfied with very little, who thought more of gain than of the comforts and luxuries of daily life,—people pertaining to good families, nevertheless, but who passed their time shooting and hunting in the country over their own lands. Sometimes, however, they were also inhabited by upstarts, who endeavoured to enrich themselves by arts and trades. The grandfather of Messer Lapo da Castiglionchio, who lived on the threshold of Messer Riccardo da Quona, beyond the Colonnine, which now stand in the Via dei Benci, and where at that time was one of the city gates, used to have this gate closed for him every night by an old woman, a good faithful servant, who afterwards deposited the key for him in his bedroom, so primitive were the manners.

But Florence meanwhile was gradually growing as the prosperity of her citizens augmented. The old houses with thatched roofs were often burnt down. When a fire broke out, the whole population was excited and every one had to be under arms and on guard. Even the Signoria, to destroy with the least expense the houses of their adversaries whom they had perchance banished from the city, used to set them aflame and then pay the damages the fire might have caused to innocent neighbours. And passions burnt as hotly as fire. The quarrels, riots, feuds, *vendette*, that were incessant, dyed the streets red with blood, while the triumphs in these frays were celebrated with feasts and banqueting. The Commune, grown proud and haughty, quickly offended, too, and ready to strike, redoubled its forces in order to subdue its foes. This achieved, the merchants of the conquering city celebrated a new species of triumph; they led their mules, laden with the cloths of Calimara, the silks of Por Santa Maria, across the plains and mountains that a short time before had been scoured by the horse and foot soldiers of their army. The traders, following hard upon the footsteps of their less peaceable neighbours, bore the gold of Florence and its manufactures to the city, under whose walls had but lately waved the banner that bore the symbolic ensign of this great free people.

The Mercato Vecchio was then the heart of Florence, and seemed to the Florentines the most beautiful piazza in the world. Whoever reads its

Or San Michele, with the old shrine. (Miniature in the *Biadajolo*).

praises in the pages of Antonio Pucci, or searches among the tales of Franco Sacchetti for the chronicles of daily life, can form an idea of a life that

A view of the demolished Ancient Market.

was contented to enact itself upon so small a stage. Here, on this, the true emporium of Florentine commerce, were gathered together shopkeepers, merchants, doctors, idlers, gamblers, rustics, apothecaries, rogues, maid-servants, courtiers, beggars, hucksters, and gay bands of spendthrifts. Here, too, was to be found merchandise of every sort and kind; fresh meat, fruit, cheese, vegetables, game, poultry, linen, flowers, pottery, barrels, and second-hand furniture. The street-boys, mischievous and quick-tongued even then, took up their permanent abode there, as if it were their proper home; here, too, rats held perpetual carnival. In short, people and things from all parts of the then known globe were gathered together in this tiny space.

No day passed that some disturbance did not occur, some quarrel, some alarm. Thus a horse became obstreperous, and every person shouted at the top of their voices for help, " Accorr'uomo "; the Piazza dei Signori was filled up with the runaways, the palace-door was hastily shut, the family armed itself, and so did the followers of the captain and of the executioner; some for very fear hid under their beds, to come out after the tumult had subsided covered with dirt and cobwebs. Two mules picked at by crows would begin to kick and jump over the stalls of the sellers. Once again all the shops were hastily shut, and

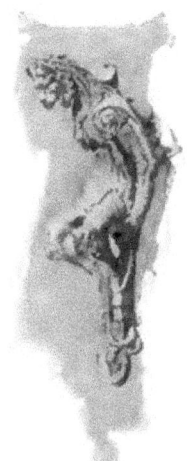

The Devil
by *Giambologna.*

serious quarrels would arise between the linen-drapers and the butchers on account of the harm done by these infuriated beasts. Sometimes even graver disputes arose. Gamblers and keepers of gaming-tables would come to blows and such a scene be enacted as is represented in the fresco in the Monastery of Lecceto near Siena. The dice fall on the table in such a manner that one of the players loses; he springs to his feet infuriated by the stroke of ill-luck, and stretching out his arms clutches the winner by the throat; the other, pale with fear and anger, seeks in vain for the avenging knife; oaths break out from the lips of the combatants; the voices of the bystanders, women and children, rise up in fear, "Accorr'uomo." The dense crowd retreats, and when the executioner arrives with his followers, always too late of course—justice, then as now, was never up to time—the victim already lies on the ground in a pool of blood.

Such the dramas, the *faits divers*, of those days, which every now and again disturbed the peace of our ancestors. The burgher story-tellers who fulfilled the office of our modern newspapers rarely tell of these cruel acts. They prefer to dwell on the tricks and practical jokes with which

the merry folk amused themselves, eternal source
of fireside talk when the housemates were gathered together before the andirons of those huge
open hearths, under whose blackened chimneys
the family assembled before the hour of putting
out the lights should sound, after which whosoever went last to bed would ascertain that the
barrels were well closed and the doors and windows tightly shut. They were always ready for
a laugh, these people—always ready to forget the
terrors of the other world held up to them by
their priests and calculated by their weird hor-
rors to damp the most buoyant spirits. The incredulity of the new age already began to peep
forth, mocking at the priests, and also a little
at the miracles and many like impostures. The
mockers and scoffers who laughed at others, and
sought to deceive their neighbours and the world,
called themselves " new men," and their mischievous doctrines " new things." The group of people that gathered around the counters of shops
and under the *loggie* that nestled close to the
palaces, made the place re-echo with their clear
silvery laughter, to which the knot of whispering
women corresponded, who clustered chatting beside their housedoors.

The artists, or, as they then called themselves, the artificers, were the most ingenious plotters of practical jokes, concocted between one stroke of the brush and another. The memory of them endured for a long while, so much so that Vasari has incorporated into his Lives various of those which the novelists had not consigned into their chronicles of citizen life. "It has ever been that among painters are found new men," says Sacchetti, — and Bonamico Buffalmacco, immortalised in the 'Decamerone,' and the names of Bartolo Gioggi, Bruno di Giovanni, Filippo di Ser Brunellesco, Paolo Uccello, and Donatello, recall to our memories tricks played on a certain Calandrino and on the Fat Carpenter, besides many others who were the victims of these merciless high spirits. But the mad wish to joke and laugh was caught also by grander people, and from the workshops of artificers it entered into those of the apothecaries, it took possession of the doctors, of the judges, of the proctors, it even climbed up into the Palace to enliven the dullness of the Priori obliged to stay here shut up far away from wife and child, simple men of simple habits, both men and habits bearing the stamp of ancient boorishness. Thus the whole

Signoria slept in one room, a fact that gave occasion for many jokes, that indeed provoked them. So simple, truly, were these *signori*, that it was not uncommon for the provost of the Priori to go himself into the kitchen to broil his own slice of meat. The tricks and pranks played bordered often, it must be owned, on roguery; but a good laugh at the expense of the person who was in the wrong, and on whom the joke had been perpetrated, was considered to put everything square. For in these days, when everybody thought of themselves and of their own interests, public opinion had no pity or compassion on the man who let himself be befooled. By common consent all manner of wily tricks were permitted to merchants, and the Florentine traders were famous for their great cunning. Sacchetti tells what happened to a certain Soccebonel of Friuli who went to buy some cloth from one of them. The merchant measured out four canes, but then managed to steal half the amount; to cover the fraud, he said to Soccebonel, "If you want to do well with this cloth, leave it to soak all night in water and you will see how excellent it will become." Soccebonel did as he was told, and then took the cloth to the shearer. When he went to fetch it back, he asked how much he had to pay. " It seems to me, nine *braccia,*" said the shearer; " therefore give me nine *soldi.*" " Nine *braccia,*" said the other, " alas! they measure, but the cloth does not grow under their hands." Soccebonel runs to the cutter, runs hither and thither, in his despair. At last he is told that these Florentine cloths do not grow in water, and one man tells him about a person who bought a *braccio* of Florentine cloth, kept it in water, and by next morning it had shrunk so that there was none left.

But whoever searches the mercantile codes amidst the dust of libraries and archives will find that they all concur in condemning such tricks. All of these papers, each of which begins, " In the name of the Father, Amen," are pervaded by instances of good examples, and all breathe excellent customs, wise saws, and honest rules. Their theoretical precepts were clearly inspired by the most severe morality. One of these sapient scribes says: —

" Bear well in mind that when you pronounce a sentence you go on straightforwardly, loyally, and justly, and do not let yourself be swayed aside from this either by bribes, love, or fear,

by relationship or friendship, or for the sake of a companion. For the person against whom you give your sentence will be your enemy, and he whom you would serve will hold you neither honest, nor loyal, nor straightforward; he will, instead, always distrust and despise you." Immediately after, a little below, we read: — " If you have need in trade or in any other business of the friendship of any lord or proprietor, I advise that with carefully chosen presents you curry his favour; watch those who are of his household, above all his secretary, and make friends with him; you can present him with some little thing to his taste, asking help and counsel of him that he may teach you how best to find favour in his master's eyes." Nor is this all. Our practical moralist gives yet another useful counsel: — " When you buy oats, look out that the measure is not filled too quickly, for it will always sink two or three per cent; but when you sell, fill quickly and your oats will grow.... Always speak well of the members of the Commune; live in charity with your neighbours, because they always are the first to speak of your affairs, and in honour or dishonour they may make or mar you."

It was thus these men of yore counselled their sons, who grew up quick-witted and expert in the art of living amid a people who were learned in all the stratagems and wiles of life. What marvel, then, that a preacher, in order to attract a congregation, and not to speak his words to the desert air, announced that he would proclaim from the pulpit that usury is not a sin? And so he did all through Lent and on Palm-Sunday to a large and attentive congregation. What we moderns term "log-rolling" was the order of the day. Families widened their borders and strengthened their connections by this means, usually favoured by matrimonial alliances, for capital was the one and only basis of safety, and this was upheld by a whole mass of laws and privileges. The father was the despot master of all his personal property. He could leave it to whomsoever he chose, to collateral relations or to some pious foundation, nay, even to those children whom love had brought into his house; and this he could do by will, a matter now impossible in continental countries, though still possible in England, where the 'Code Napoléon' does not obtain. From this fact we can realise the important place that lawyers and clerks then occupied, for disputes about testaments were quite common occurrences. A wife inheriting *ab intestato* had a right only to a fourth of her children's goods, and in reality only to mere nourishment. Everything conspired to preserve the integrity of capital and prevent it from leaving the family, the firm, and the commune. It is a point that cannot be too much insisted on. Inside that society of merchants a greed for gain was the supreme law of every action. It would be useless to look for the sentiment that inspires the modern family, where for woman is reserved so noble a *rôle*, such honourable and tender offices. Those poor Florentine mothers had to be contented with such humble activity as the tyranny of their husbands permitted to them, and to live, or rather to drag out, their lives in those gloomy squalid houses, taking care of the children, visiting the churches, and confessing to the friars their manifold sins of desire. The daughters—those girls with whom to-day we take such pains—were then never even taught to read. "If it is a girl, put her to sew and not to read; it is not good that a woman should know how to read unless you wish to make her a nun," thus counsels Paolo di Ser

Pace da Certaldo. The convents were then, and for centuries after, the sole refuge for these poor wretches. They were also a providence for prolific families. To have twenty or more children seemed the most natural thing in the world. If they lived it was said, "Heaven be praised;" and if they died, "For everything be Heaven praised, Amen." Such were the sentiments of the times. In the memoranda, in domestic chronicles in the time of great mortality, were registered in such terms the deaths as well as the births, with a serenity that to-day to loving mothers would seem cynicism indeed.

These documents also hand down to us indisputable proofs of a singular fact—that is, the intrusion in the family of a new element that obscures the vaunted purity of the morals of those past days. Benevolent critics find an excuse for this because of the great void made by the plague among the city and country dwellers, and because the prospect of small wages was not enough to induce the men and women of the people to go out as domestic servants; hence it was necessary to look to foreign commerce to supply the deficiency. But this reasoning hardly holds. Rather we think it was the trade with the East, the vagabond life led by the merchants, and their ever-increasing wealth, that caused that traffic in slaves of both sexes which lasted through two centuries, from the beginning of the thirteenth century onwards. Oriental slaves bought as live goods, generally through Genoese, Venetian, and Neapolitan brokers, were chiefly Tartars, Greeks, Turks, Dalmatians, and Circassians, and do not seem to have been archetypes of beauty. The registers in which the notaries marked down, together with the name and age, the price and description of the wares, " the points " of the necks and faces of the slaves bought and sold, bear witness to this circumstance; nearly all had olive complexions, though some were found who had rosy skins and were florid and fair. The faces never seemed to lack some special and distinctive mark—some were pocked, some had moles, others were scarred; the nose was generally squat and flat, the lips thick and prominent, the eyes dull and small, the foreheads low and freckled. To these pen-sketches made by pedantic and precise lawyers some portraits correspond that are still extant of these women. In a rare and curious book, the memoranda of Baldovinetti, in which this ancestor of the famous painter used to illustrate by drawings his journalistic jottings, there are preserved for us the portraits of three slaves he bought in the years 1377, 1380, 1388: "Dorothea, a Tartar, from Russia, eighteen years or more of age; Domenica, of white skin, from Tartary; and Veronica, sixteen years old, whom I bought almost naked from Bonaroti, son of Simon de Bonaroti" — that is to say, from an ancestor of Michael Angelo. These three — Dorothea, Domenica and Veronica — could, when a little older, have easily served as models to the future Buonarroti for his "Three Fates." Such women, ugly or beautiful, entered the houses of the rich Florentines to perform the most humble services and to take care of the children. They caused much anxiety on every account to the poor house matrons. Pucci, in one of his sonnets, tells us that the slaves had the best of it in everything, and were above every good match, checkmating their masters. He maliciously explains some reasons, and tells that they often knew how to play ugly tricks on their mistresses, who, as Alessandra Macinghi, the mother of the Strozzi, confessed some years later, would avenge themselves by laying hand on these same slaves. Still, pests though they were, it seems the families could not do without them. They were the nurses, the maids-of-all-work, of their day; and Alessandra wrote to her son Filippo when at Naples: "Let me remind you of the need we have of a slave, for so for we have always had one. If you give orders to have one bought, ask for a Tartar, for they are the best for hard work, and are simple in their ways. The Russians are more delicate and prettier, but according to my judgment a Tartar would be best." Nor could Madonna Alessandra have found any one who could execute her commission better than Filippo, who already had with him for a long while a slave who knew how to work well, and about whom his mother wrote, April 7th, 1469: "Andrea as well as Tomaso Ginori, who are now with you, came to see us on Easter Day, and told me many things about your household, and especially about Marina, and the many pretty ways she has with you." And a year later, in an ironical tone, she says, "I send you the towels; be careful that Madama Marina does not make them disappear," from which we gather that by cunning and pretty ways these women knew how to win over their masters and become madam.

Fresco in the Monastery of Lecceto near Siena.

They even obtained, by faithful labour, good behaviour, and general aptitude, many a liberal testamentary bequest. It was yet worse when that bartered blood of Tartars and Russians mixed with that of this pure, ancient, and free race.

But let us return to the chaster atmosphere of the family, in which, with accumulated riches, there entered also, alas! those poisonous germs which later on were destined to corrupt and corrode Italian life and conscience. Between the fourteenth and fifteenth centuries a great change occurred. The renovation of manners and customs, already panting towards a freer life, that became entirely unbridled in the Renaissance, had weakened faith and discouraged religion. It seemed as though the people no longer understood any but worldly pleasures. The letters of Mazzei, the good notary of Prato, the wise man of "rough soul and frozen heart," bear witness to this. Ser Lapo was an ascetic spirit, a man of good and ancient faith, and a convinced moralist. In his letters is reflected the rebellious sinner, struggling against the holier tendencies that seek to lead him to a peaceful death and the redemption of his earthly errors. It is the fight between the religious sentiment and the moralistic spirit of the new age that radiated in the glory of the Renaissance, but which, after a wonderful moment of splendour, left behind it in the souls of Italians a black and deadly void. Out of this darkness the modern man was to arise later on, purified by these centuries of servitude, and matured by many vigils of thought.

But we have again wandered from the family. Let us look in once more upon the Florentine house, out of whose windows " the loving slaves shook the dust from their masters' dress every morning, looking fresher and happier than the rose," as a poem of the period has it—this house where the wife barely passed in happiness even the very first months of her married life: later on she merely numbered the years that sped by the names of the children who grew up around her, each of whom recalled to her one of her husband's long absences, when he had gone away to trade far off beyond the mountains and over the seas. The youthful freshness of these women faded quickly, and as Sacchetti writes, the most beautiful among them in a short time " drooped, degenerated, withered in old age, and at last became a skull." It was but natural that they should try to correct nature by art, and repair the ravages induced by domestic cares; and this not merely from vanity. Even great painters like Taddeo Gaddi and Alberto Arnoldi agreed that the Florentine women were the best artists of all the world.

" Was there ever before them a painter—nay, even a mere dyer—who could turn black into white? Certainly not; for it is against nature. Yet, if a face is yellow and pallid, they change it by artificial means to the hue of the rose. One who by nature or age has a skinny figure, they are able to make florid and plump. I do not think Giotto or any other painter could colour better than they do; but the most wonderful thing is that even a face which is out of proportion and has goggle eyes, they will make correct with eyes like to a falcon's. As to crooked noses, they are soon put straight. If they have jaws like a donkey, they quickly correct them. If their shoulders are too large, they plane them; if one projects more than the other, they stuff them so with cotton that they seem in proportion. And so on with breasts and hips, doing all this without a scalpel, so that Polycletus himself could not have rivalled them. The Florentine women are past-mistresses of painting and modelling, for it is plain to see that they restore where nature has failed."

We cannot blame them, nor do we wish to do so. Poor women! this was the only freedom they enjoyed, to masquerade as youthful, happy creatures, to make their faces bright and fresh while their hearts were often weeping at finding themselves supplanted by other women. They also loved to change the fashion and shape of the dresses, and here they were able to give free vent to that ambitious spirit which they possessed no less than their male relatives. The admirers of the past, beginning with Dante, blame them for so much volubility, which irritated even the story-tellers and priests, not to mention the husbands, who would willingly have economised on these extravagant expenses of their wives. Sacchetti had much to say on this theme, over which he grows eloquent. He writes in his virtuous indignation how "some women had their dresses cut so low that the armpit could be seen. They then gave a jump and made the collars come up to their ears. The girls who used to go about so modestly have entirely changed the shape of their hood, so as to reduce it to a cap, and with this headgear they wear around their necks a collar to which are attached all sorts of little beasts that hang down into their breasts. As for their sleeves, they can almost be called mattresses. Was there ever invented a more harmful, useless shape? Could a woman wearing those things lift a glass or whatever else from the table with-out soiling both sleeve and table-cloth, not to mention the tumblers they upset? Their waists, too, are all squeezed in, their arms are covered by their trains, and their throats enclosed with hoods. One would never end if one wished to say everything about these women, beginning with their immeasurable trains. Then their heads are dressed high and reach up to the roofs; some curl their hair, some plaster it down, and some others powder it. It is enough to make one sick."

It would seem, however, that this craving for the new attacked men as well, and was by no means confined to the weaker sex. Poor Messer Valore di Buondelmonte, an old man cut on the ancient pattern, was forced by his relations to change his hood. Everybody marvelled and stopped him in the street. "Oh, what! is this

Messer Valore? I do not know you. What is the matter with you? Have you the mumps?"

At one time it was the fashion to wear such ruffs and wrist-bands that it could be said of the Florentines that they wore water-pipes around their necks and tiles on their arms; whence it happened that Salvestro Brunelleschi, while eating peas with a spoon, instead of putting them into his mouth, put them inside his ruff, and scalded himself. Later on it became fashionable to have the hose divided and crossed in three or four colours. Shoes had very long points, and the legs were so swathed with strings that the wearer could hardly sit down. Most of the youths went without a mantle, and wore their hair down to their shoulders. For the wrist-band a *braccio* of cloth was allowed, and more stuff was put in a glove than in a hood. The old fashions struggled with the new, the newer, the very newest. Everybody was individually capricious. The Florentine people, inquisitive then as now, liked to behold the new dresses, mantles and gabardines in which their townsfolk were muffled, so that they hardly recognised each other and had to scan one another keenly in the face before friend knew friend.

It was a veritable masquerade. They finally assumed such proportions that the men, who have always been the law-makers, pondered how they could by legislation put a check upon the " extravagant ornament of the Florentine women." In 1306 and 1333 the Commune promulgated sumptuary laws, reinforced in 1352, 1355, 1384, 1388, 1396, when very severe regulations were added. These had again to be revived in 1439, 1456, and once more in 1562. The clergy thundered from the pulpits, the wise men admonished, and some of them went the length of furnishing regulations to careful mothers about their own dress and that of their daughters. The story-tellers lashed with their wit this immoderate luxury — the result, as they maintained, of female vanity. Meanwhile the other cities of Tuscany and Italy sent to the Florentine merchants for samples " of the above named goods" and constantly repeated their orders, showing that Florence set the fashion in those days, and that its extravagance in habiliments was eagerly copied outside its walls. At the same time there began a curious contest between the severity of the rigorous legislation and the cunning of the women. These astute ladies did not fight openly; they pretended to bow their heads and merely appear annoyed, while in reality they waited for the storm to pass. They were too wise; they knew the world too well not to be aware that laws which are too severe remain ever a dead letter. Whenever and howsoever they could, they sought, if not to annul, at least to elude them. Thus, when the Duke of Calabria came to Florence in 1326, the ladies gathered round the duchess, who was a Frenchwoman, Marie de Valois, and obtained from her the concession that a certain thick yellow-and-white silk braid, which they had worn instead af plaits of hair in front of their faces, should be restored to them. "An immodest and unnatural ornament," grumbles Villani, who had observed how the inordinate appetite of women triumphs over reasonable and wise men. Four years after, on the 1st of April 1330, the Florentines deprived their women of every ornament. But even this tempest blew over. Like the women of Flanders, of whom Paradin writes in the 'Annales de Bourgogne,' when tormented for the same cause by Thomas Cornette, a fanatical Carmelite, they "relèverent leur cornes, et firent comme les lymaçons, lesquels quand ils entendent quelque bruit retirent et resserrent tout bellement leurs cornes; mais, le bruit passé, soudain ils les relèvent plus grandes que devant." And an occasion to put forth their horns anew was the coming af the Duke of Athens to Florence in 1342, when the French wore " such wonderfully different dresses," as a contemporary chronicler observes. These were the days when young men clothed themselves in such tight and short kilts that in order to put them on they had to be helped by another person— kilts that were belted in at the waist by a band of leather, closed by a rich buckle, from which they appended a fancifully worked German purse. Their hood was joined on to a short mantle, and ended in a long peak that reached to the ground and which they were able to wrap round their heads when cold. The cavaliers wore close-fitting jackets, with the points of the wrist-band lined with miniver or ermine, reaching to the floor. Of course the women immediately copied this new caprice. In the frescoes attributed to Simone Memmi in Santa Maria Novella, we can behold these fashions, which had then but just come in, and whence we can gather a faint conception of the magnificent material employed in the making of these gorgeous garments. The pragmatical laws of dress, dating from 1343, which are preserved in the Archivio della Grascia, tell of splendid dresses that were sequestered by the rigour of the law, and marked by the servants of these unfortunate foreign officers chosen by the Commune to apply the laws, with a seal of lead, having on one side half a lily, and on the other half a cross. Here is the description of a forbidden gown which belonged to Donna Francesca, the wife of Landozzo di Uberto degli Albizi, of the parish of San Pietro Maggiore: "A black mantle of raised cloth; the ground is yellow, and over it are woven birds, parrots, butterflies, white and red roses, and many figures in vermilion and green, with pavilions and dragons, and yellow and black letters and trees, and many other figures of various colours—the whole lined with cloth in hues of black and vermilion."

Often instead of letters they had whole proverbs embroidered on their dresses. In those same archives they keep a curious document, telling of those unlucky officials who were obliged to fulfil a duty so ungracious — of those poor *podestà* and captains, cavaliers, judges, notaries, and servants, who came to Florence from the Guelph cities of Lombardy and the Marches to hold the office of governors, and who had to dispute in their rough dialect with the quick tongues of the Florentine women and their husbands, and were laughed at for their pains by the story-tellers of the city. There is a tale told by Franco Sacchetti narrating the sufferings of a judge, Messer Amerigo Amerighi of Pesaro, " in person most beautiful, and able in his science, " who was ordered, while Franco was one of the Priori, to proceed with solicitude to execute certain orders, as usual on the ornaments of the women. The valiant judge set to work, sending around notaries and servants to make the requisite inquisition; but the citizens went up to the Signoria and said that the new *podestà* did his work so well, that never before had the women been so free to dress as they pleased as they were now. Here is the justification of the unfortunate Messer Amerigo: —

"My Lords, I have studied all my life, and now, when I thought that I knew something, I find that I know nothing. For, looking out for these ornaments of your women, which, according to your orders, are forbidden, such arguments as they brought forward in their defence I have never before heard, and from among them I should like to mention to you a few. There comes a woman with the point of her hood peaked and twisted round. My notary says, 'Tell me your name, because your point is peaked.' The good woman takes down the point, which is fastened to the hood with a pin, and, holding it in her hand, says, 'Why, no; do you not see it is a wreath?' Then my man goes farther, and finds a woman wearing many buttons in front of her dress. He tells her that she cannot wear all those buttons. She answers, 'Yes, Messere, I can wear these; they are not buttons, and if you do not believe me look for the hanks, and see, too, that there are no buttonholes.' The notary goes to another, who wears ermine, wondering what she will have to say for herself. 'You wear ermine,' he remarks, and is about to put down her name. The woman says, 'Do not put down my name, because these are not ermine. This is the fur of a suckling.' 'What is this suckling?' asks the notary, and the woman answers, 'It is an animal.'"

The notary does not insist, nor can the Signoria, who, remembering their own women at home, conclude, as they have always concluded at the Palace, by exhorting Messer Amerigo to let things be, to allow the women to pass their false buttons, their suckling's fur, and their belts. They do not wish perhaps that the judge from Pesaro should remember the melancholy distich that one of his colleagues of the guild of merchants had written on the margin of his sumptuary statutes:—

> "If there is a person you do hate,
> Send him to Florence as officer of State."

Once again one of Sacchetti's stories proves itself a truthful historical document. The Archivio della Grascia preserves the acts of the Judge of Appeal and Cassation. Among these protocols is one written by Giovanni di Piero da Lugo, notary under Ser Amerigo of Pesaro, officer of the Grascia to the Commune of Florence for six months, beginning from March 15th, 1384. On that day Amerigo issued a proclamation to recall to memory the punishment inflicted by the law against whomsoever transgressed the sumptuary regulations. On the 27th of March the inquisition on the part of the officials began. When they met a woman with two rings ornamented with four pearls, or wearing a little cap embroidered, or a wreath, or too many buttons on her dress, immediately the unlucky creature was noted down as being in contravention, to use a modern phrase. The sergeant would go to her house with a summons for her to appear before the judge. On the day appointed her husband would put in an appearance on behalf of his wife, who, recognising the error, paid the fine. These things went on for a good while. Later on the women, grown malicious, began those contests recounted with such evident gusto by the story-tellers, but naturally omitted in the protocols of the notary. The inquisitions grew more rare, the sentences less frequent, and those husbands who appeared before the tribunals began to deny the guilt of their wives with valid arguments. One is too old to be capable of what is imputed to her, another was at home on that day and at that hour, a third is in mourning—and so forth. The protocol is closed with hardly a sentence registered, the real fact being that the Signoria and the judges above all, had given themselves up as vanquished—a defeat that is not devoid of the suspicion that those officers and notaries chosen for this hateful magisterial office had allowed themselves to be conquered by the fire of some beautiful eyes and the caresses of some flattering voice. For inside the cover of a copy of the pragmatic or sumptuary laws of that date still extant in the Florentine archives, do not we read the outpourings of some enamoured heart which proves itself a precious human document embedded among the pedantic quibbles? This is how it runs:—

> "The troops of merry friends, the songs so sweet,
>   The hawks, the hounds, the wanderings full of pleasure,
> Fair women temples, where for love my feet
>   Were wont on holidays to seek my treasure,
> I hate them now, like fire. This thought I meet
>   Where'er I go,—oh, wretched beyond measure!
> Thou dwellest far from me, my love, my own,
>   My sovereign hope, and I am here alone."

Is this not proof enough to show that the women had found partisans in the very bosom of the magistracy? No wonder their cause was won. But for a short time only, because periodically some fresh charge was made against feminine vanity, and other storms broke out. The poor women, they were really much persecuted! They also encountered terrible adversaries in the moralists of the day, who in their tractates concerning the government of the family did not cease striking that note. Palmieri is an example of this. Their worst foes, however, were the friars, at that time invaded by a furious desire to purge the world of its sins. Fra Bernardino of Siena, in 1425, continued in Perugia those bonfires of all the worldly vanities that he had initiated the year before in Rome, making great havoc of false hair and other vain adornments, of trimming and hoods, of dice, cards, gaming-tables, and other such diabolic things, foreshadowing the great fires made by Savonarola in Florence in 1497, that proved of such evil omen to their instigator. Nevertheless, among so many foes staunch partisans were not wanting. In April 1461, a preacher who had shouted in Santa Croce against the women, also appealed against them in the presence of the Signoria, in the Consiglio dei Richiesti, where no less a matter was discussed than the absolute prohibition of all fashion. On this occasion Luigi Guicciardini, father of the great historian and politician, said that he had replied to a Milanese who drew evil deductions as to the morality of the Florentine women from their extravagant dress, that if the dress seemed immodest their acts were far different.

But these sumptuary laws, retouched and re-manipulated every now and again, were less onerous to the women than to their husbands, whose purses had to pay the fines. Nor were the regulations confined to the limiting of personal adornment. The luxury and pomp permitted at weddings, baptisms, banquets, and funerals were all rigorously laid down. Thus the number of guests at a marriage could not exceed 200; the marriage-brokers had to announce beforehand the names of the guests. The marriage portions were also fixed by law, as well as the nuptial ceremonies. The cook who prepared the wedding dinner was obliged to report to the officers of the Commune the number of dishes which he served. The meats might not be more than three; not more than seven pounds of veal; and the number of capons, turkeys, ducks was also minutely stated in the statutes. So also were the rites to be observed at obsequies, the number of wax torches that might be burned, the clothes the dead were permitted to wear, the dresses of those that followed them; the presents permitted at baptisms: in short, every single little thing that occurred in the daily life of the citizens was minutely and carefully regulated, and

whosoever disobeyed these regulations was condemned to pay a heavy fine; for even in those days the municipal government eagerly seized on every excuse in order to tax its citizens, and the study of those citizens, especially of those cunning merchants, was in every possible way to lighten for themselves by circumvention the burden of these imposts,—in fact, to use a phrase of the period, " to steal with honest licence."
" The Commune steals so much itself, I may as well steal from it also," is an old saying quoted by Sacchetti, who laments the slow procedure of the Commune even towards those who desire to give up to it their goods. " Everybody drew water for their own mill," says Marchionne Stefani, and he too had his own mill to work. They all strove to defend themselves from these charges; " and as it always happens," writes the chronicler, " the heavy large beasts jump and break the nets." Thus Francesco Datini, when dealing with those who ruled the State, took care of number one. In those years when it was necessary that the imposts should be levied ten or fifteen times a year, on account of the wars fought by the arms of the mercenaries and because of the treaties of peace concluded by

means of money, whosoever could not accomplish what he wanted by the aid of friendship or favours, arrived at his goal by cunning, like Bartolo Sonaglini, who, when he was about to be heavily taxed, used to go down every morning and stand on the threshold of his own door narrating his evil fortunes and financial difficulties to everybody who passed by, saying, " O brother, I am ruined! I must either disappear from the world or die in prison; " so that when the time came to tax him everybody said, " He is impoverished and will be taken up for debt; " and one said, " He speaks truth, for one morning he did not even dare to come out of his house; " and another remarked, " So he said to me; " and, " Well, if it be so, one must treat him as if he were poor," was the universal decision. Consequently all of one accord lent to him as if he were a beggar or worse. Having thus borrowed, and the danger passed, Bartolo once more began to come out of his house, saying that he was arranging with his creditors; and in this wise, with much talk, he freed himself of his debts, while many others richer than he were ruined.

The times were ripening. Of the ancient proverbial simplicity amid all this great thirst for gain there only remained as living monuments a few old men greatly respected. Of these Velluti has preserved to us a graphic description that is as living and vigorous as one of the figures painted by Andrea del Castagno:—

"Buonaccorso di Piero was a valiant strong patriot, and very sure in arms. He performed many a bold and noble deed, whether for his own commune or that of others. So many wounds had he received in wars and fights that he was disfigured by numberless scars. He was of good height, strong-limbed and well built. He lived a full one hundred and twenty years, but in the last twenty he was blind from old age. Although he was so old, his fibre was so tough that he could not be thrown, and by taking a young man by the shoulders he could make him sit down. He thoroughly understood all matters of trade and did everything loyally. It was believed that many cloths that came from Milan, of which a great number were ordered, and which were sold before the bales were opened, were dyed here; and I heard a certain agent, Giovanni del Volpe, seeing that the cloth sold so well, thought of saving for his firm by dyeing in a cheaper and inferior way, so that after a while these cloths were not so much sought after as before. Inquiring into the reason, it was discovered that it was owing to the cunning of Giovanni; and Buonaccorso hearing of this, wanted to kill him. Buonaccorso having lost his sight, mostly stopped at home. Behind his palace in Via Maggio there was a long balcony which went the length of the building, and on this opened three rooms. Here he walked up and down so much every morning that he covered three or four miles. After this he broke his fast with no less than two loaves; then at dinner he ate well, for he was a hearty eater; and so he passed his life. Now as to how he died: I heard my father say that wanting to go to the fireplace he hit his foot against it, and so sprained his ankle that he could no longer take his daily exercise on the balcony, after which he then and there declared himself dead. Now it happened that his son Filippo, my grandfather, took in second marriage Monna Gemma dei Pulci; and Buonaccorso, having that day chatted much, twitting his son, saying that he needed a wife to help him more than he did, and much more such talk, expressed a wish to go from his bed to his lounge; so he called my father and Gerardo his grandson, and as he put his arms round their necks and shoulders to raise himself, suddenly by reason of great age his life failed him and he died."

With the memory of this beloved and good patriarchal image fresh in our minds, let us hurry on to the new era and the new century, whose glorious dawn already gilded the sky of literature and art. The preliminary signs had made themselves felt in the growth of wealth, in the enfranchisement from the old prejudices as well as from the severe rules of the old way of living, in the egotistical tendencies which prepared the way for the evolution of what we moderns call individualism. By all these signs and tokens we recognise the character of the men and the life of the Renaissance. The affection for a common country and even family was weakened by an acute craving for pleasure; incredulity, scepticism and sensuality threatened to obtain the upper hand. After the passing away of the dread terrors of the plague, these generations must almost have wondered to find themselves alive. From the great beginning of the mortality of 1348 to the early years of the fifteenth century, the chroniclers register no less than six such epidemics, though some were of comparatively minor deadliness. By consulting the books of death preserved in the archives of the Grascia, it is possible to ascertain that from the 1st of May to the 18th of September 1400 there occurred no fewer than 10,908 deaths, of which the greater part were children. Of the plague of 1348, besides the classical and splendid description of Boccaccio, we can discover vivid and sad records amid the family chronicles in the diaries and memoranda of the day. It must have been a despairing and awe inspiring sight. Giovanni Morelli tells us how in one hour a friend or neighbour was laughing and joking, and the next he was dead. People fell down dead in the streets and at their benches; fell down dead when alone, without the help or comfort of a human being. Many went mad and threw themselves into the wells or the Arno, or from out their windows, driven to this by great sorrow or panic or fear. Many and many died unseen, many were buried before the breath had left their bodies. One might see the cross-bearing priests who had gone to fetch a corpse take up two or three on their way to the church. It is calculated that in Florence alone two-thirds of the population died—that, is 18,000 persons. Of the epidemic of 1400 a detailed description is given in a letter of Ser Lapo Mazzei: " Here shops are hardly open any more; the masters are not at their desks; the police, the justice is without superiors. No one weeps for the dead." It was an awful visitation; children died, friends, neighbours, and relations fell victims; there was no longer any means of recording even the names of the dead. The number of victims who were struck down in the summer alone reached the figure of one hundred a day, and on one day in July it rose to no fewer than two hundred. Of the epidemic of 1420, Gregorio Dati writes in his ' Libro Segreto '—that is to say, his diary:—

"The pestilence was in our house. It began with the man-servant Piccino, about 1420. Within three days later our slave Martha died. On the 1st of April my daughter Sandra and on the 5th Antonia. We left the house and went into one opposite. In a few days Veronica died. Again we moved and went to live in Via Chiara. Here Vandecca and Pippa were taken ill, and on the 1st of August both went to heaven. They all died of the plague. Heaven help them!"

Those who could, ran away to Arezzo, Bologna, Romagna, or any city or country where they thought they would be safe. It was the rule to go to any place where the plague had already been. Remedies against the mysterious sickness there seemed to be none. Morelli lays down some rules that to-day would be called hygienic: —

"The pestilence of 1348 was caused by a terrible famine. The year before, it happened that in Florence there was great hunger; we lived on herbs and reeds, and very bad they were; all the country was full of people, who went about feeding on grass like beasts. The corpses were disposed of in any mode, and there was no help for this."

This chronicler counsels people to keep themselves in good condition; to be careful to eat well and avoid damp; to spend generously and without stint or economy; to refrain from melancholy and gloom; not to think of dull sorrowful things; to play, ride, amuse themselves, be happy.

The survivors from the scourge must have quickly accustomed themselves to the tenor of the new life, once the danger was over. One result of the plague was the institution of processions of "white penitents," resembling those which in the previous century traversed all Europe under the name of "The Company of the Crushed." Folk left their homes in crowds, both men and women, laymen and ecclesiastics, all mingling together, dressed in white cloaks which covered their faces and wearing a crucifix as their badge. They walked in procession from place to place, singing lauds and supplicating *Misericordia* in loud voices; at night they lay in the open air, and only asked for bread and water. The people of the cities they visited caught their fervour and went in like order to visit other towns. On the appearance of these pious pilgrims every one was moved to repentance; enmities were laid aside, discordant factions were filled with sanctity. Some vicious persons in Florence sought to profit by this agitation and liberate the prisoners from the *Stinche*, but fortunately they were hindered. Francesco Datini, a merchant from Prato and a great benefactor to his town, though otherwise a man of dubious morality, who ill-treated his wife and preferred his slave in her presence, also went on a pilgrimage in August 1399, dressed in white linen and barefooted, together with his family, friends, and neighbours. They were twelve in all, and had with them two horses and a mule. On these beasts they put two trunks in which were boxes filled with all

The prisons *Le Stinche*. (From an engraving in Politian's *Conjurationis Pactianae Commentarium*, edited by *I. Adimari*, 1769).

manner of good things to eat—cheese of every kind, fresh bread and biscuits, plain and sweet tarts, and other such tit-bits of daily life—so much so that the beasts were quite overladen with the burden of the victuals. This pilgrimage lasted ten days, and went as far as Arezzo. Wherever they passed they bought eatables. This making of pilgrimages on horseback, well supplied with food, was certainly a gay and comfortable way of doing penance. The more intelligent and incredulous barely respected the outward forms of religion. Datini, for example, only feared the upbraidings and reproaches of his friend and spiritual mentor, Ser Lapo Mazzei. Others, like Buonaccorso Pitti, furnish us with the type of a man of the Renaissance who had no fixed residence, who wandered over the world tormented with inner restlessness; who gambled, lost, and traded; who meddled with commerce and politics, just like an adventurer of the eighteenth century, like Benvenuto Cellini, but without his art and with far less intelligence. A curious, strange type this Pitti, who seemed as though bitten by a tarantula, living by his wits, the intimate of Charles VI, of dukes and princes, who for a wager with the girl he loved rode straight away to Rome without stopping; a great dancer, an inveterate gambler, a brave and loyal cavalier, who in time rose to the highest offices. Burckhardt calls him a forerunner of Casanova; like him, journeying continually in the quality of merchant and political agent, diplomat and professional gambler, finding competitors only among princes like the Dukes of Brabant, Bavaria, and Savoy. This was the father of that Lucca Pitti who in riches and magnificence rivalled the Medici and tried in all things to vie with Cosimo.

The merchants, grown immeasurably rich, thanks to their traffic, their journeys, their visits to the factories established in all the commercial centres and ports of Europe, had developed into bankers and money lenders, feeling the times to be ripe when they could tranquilly enjoy the fruits of their exertions. Florence, like a lovely, prosperous maiden of good parts and

The *Canto dei Pazzi*, at the corner of *Borgo degli Albizi*.
(From Politian's edition, 1769).

abundant dowry, the factions quieted that had quarrelled concerning her, closed her eyes under the shade of the Medicean laurels, dazzled by the magnificence with which, womanlike, she had allowed herself to be conquered. Now that the

Consecration of the *Duomo* by Pope Eugenius 4th.
(From a Missal in the Laurentian Library).

families had acquired property, they sought to found houses, they looked out for suitable marriages, which were discussed as though they were political alliances. Alessandra Macinghi degli Strozzi went to mass every morning in Santa Reparata to sit behind the girls whom she would like her son Filippo to marry, and with the eye of a future mother-in-law studied, examined, criticised, and wrote about them to her son as though the matter in hand were a bargain about a horse. It is true that Alessandra, to our mind, has been too much exalted and praised; she must have had the heart of a merchant, not that of a woman. That she laid hands upon her slaves she frankly confesses herself. This, however, was the custom of the day; it was perhaps easy to lose one's temper with those Russians and Tartars. But concerning her charity, we have stumbled on a curious document. It regards two old people, only survivors of a family of labourers. " Piero and Monna Cilia are both alive and infirm. I have overflowed the field for next year, and as I must put it in order, these two old people, if they do not

The *Duomo*, end of the 15th century.
(From a Laurentian miniature).

die, must go and beg. Heaven will provide."
Nor is this a passing thought; it was a firm
resolve. In a letter written a few months later
we read: "Piero is still alive" (Heaven had
already provided for Monna Cilia, it seems), "so
he must put up with it and go away and beg.
It would be best, of course, if Heaven would
take him." Evidently it was not possible to
combine good farming with a good heart, and
this little incident probably reflects very truly
the sentiments of the age in which they were
uttered.

But some of those who had increased and
multiplied their means showed nobler sentiments
and finer feelings. In Giovanni Rucellai we see
the perfect type of the Florentine who appre-
ciated the dignity of the new state in which for-
tune had placed him; for he had not only the
gift of making money, he also understood how
to spend it well, no less a virtue.

"I think," he writes in his *zibaldone*, "that
it has brought me more honour to have spent
well than earned well, and brought more con-
tentment to my spirit, especially the work that
I have done in my house." He thanks Heaven
for having made him "a rational being—a Chris-

tian and not a Turk, Moor, or Tartar; and for having been born in Italy, which is the most worthy and noble portion of Christendom, and in the province of Tuscany, which is the most

The Palace of the Podestà, end of the 15th century.
(From Politian's edition, 1769).

highly respected amid the provinces of Italy, and, above all, in the city of Florence, reputed the noblest and most beautiful city, not only in Christendom, but in the whole universal world; and finally, for living in the present age, held to be, by those who know, the greatest that our city has ever seen since it was founded, as well as for living in the time of the magnificent citizen Cosimo dei Medici." He also expresses his gratitude to Heaven for having granted him the favour of becoming allied to this great man, through the marriage of his son Bernardo with Nannina, daughter of Piero and niece of Cosimo—a splendid connection, of which Rucellai was justly proud.

In those days, without fear of the sumptuary laws now fallen into disuse, Florence celebrated the nuptial feast of her great families with all the splendour she could muster. The wedding of Baccio Adimari and Lisa Ricasoli, which took place in 1420, is represented in a well-known old picture that hangs in the Florentine Academy of Fine Arts. We see the happy couple and their friends dancing to the accompaniment of trumpets and fifes under a striped awning of variegated colours. This marriage and that of the Rucellai and Medici furnish us with a graphic picture of life in those days. Fortunately, too, the great old man, in his *zibaldone*, has embalmed a record of the latter festivity in a description full of loving remembrance, which has become a precious document for the student of the manners and customs of the day. Gilded by the flaming sun of June, green festoons swung proudly across the street which was the scene of the wedding, festoons that brought into high relief the shields which ornamented the house-fronts, and which were quartered half with the arms of the Medici and half with those of the Rucellai. The rude stones of the place façade, which Giovanni Rucellai's generosity had caused him to rebuild some years before, choosing as its architect Leon Battista Alberti, acquired a new aspect thus bedecked with bright awnings and festoons that hung from the Doric pilasters of the first floor and over the Corinthian pilasters of the second and third. Opposite the palace, in the little piazza in front of the Loggia, had been erected a platform in the shape of a triangle; this was covered over to defend it from the sun by a canopy of blue cloth adorned with wreaths, between which peeped the freshest roses. Below on the wooden planks were laid tapestries, and precious tapestries also covered the benches placed round for the convenience of those who waited. .The ends of the great blue velarium hung down here and there to the ground like aerial columns. On one side of that great tent there was a large sideboard, on which glittered silver vessels and dishes wrought by the best gold and silver smiths in Florence. The richness of these adornments presaged the magnificence of the banquet that was preparing. The kitchen had been placed in the street by the side of the palace, where, counting cooks and underlings, fifty persons were at work. The noise was great; Via della Vigna was crowded with people from one end to the other. The men who had decked the façade were succeeded by the servants who carried the presents from friends, clients, and relations; peasants, gardeners and shop-people brought victuals; pipers and trumpeters were preparing their music, and the cavaliers were making ready for the tilting-match. That Sunday, June 8, 1460, soon after dawn, the crowd began to arrive from all sides at the palace where the wedding was to take place. There also came, welcome and promising sight to the curious, quartered bullocks, casks of Greek wine, and as many capons as could hang on a staff borne on the shoulders of two stout peasants; bars of buffalo-cheese, turkeys in pairs, barrels of ordinary wine and choice sweet wine, baskets full of pomegranates, hampers of large sea-fish, crates of little oilver-scaled fish from the Arno, birds, hares, cream-cheese packed in fresh green rushes, baskets full of sweetmeats, tarts, and other delicate confectionery prepared by the fair hands of some gentle nun. There advanced slowly, shaking its leafy head as it stood on the cart drawn by panting oxen, a splendid olive-tree from Carmignano, as well as young oaks procured from the Villa at Sesto, not to mention the flowers that glad season gave in such profusion. The presents, worthy of those who sent them, enhanced the magnificence of the feast, testifying to the love and reverence the donors bore towards the two illustrious families about to be allied by these nuptials. Thus by this marriage old Giovanni Rucellai did away with all suspicion of being an enemy to the Medici faction, which had grown stronger in Florence since the exile of Cosimo. It was a connection planned with much judgment and which brought as much honour to his family as the façade of Santa Maria Novella, which he caused Alberti to build, the chapel of San Pancrazio, the Palace, and the beautiful Corinthian Loggia in Via della Vigna. That majestic old man, with high open forehead, aquiline nose and piercing blue eyes that still look out at us from an old portrait, had a subtle wit. His thick black hair fell in close curls on to his shoulders, a long wavy beard rested on his breast, preserving a few gold threads mixed with the grey of years; his fresh colouring denotes a vigorous old age. We see him seated in a large armchair covered with fringed crimson velvet embossed with gold. He wears a dark green tunic covered by a purple gown with turnovers of crimson velvet; his upward-looking eyes have a far-away gaze, as though he were thinking of things not of this world. The right hand, adorned with a ring set with a large diamond, rests heavily on the arm of the chair; the left, which is open, points to a handsomely bound MS., the title of which is ' Delle Antichità.' Beside it are a few open letters with the address, "To the Illustrissimo Signor Giovanni Rucellai." Behind a dark curtain, against a blue background, are painted with much care and diligence the works he had executed in stone and marble, the front of Santa Maria Novella, the chapel of San Pancrazio, the Palace and the Loggia. Thus the picture sums up both the man and his glory, the rich merchant who had become related to Cosimo di Giovanni dei Medici.

Giovanna dei Medici came to her wedding accompanied, as was the custom, by four cavaliers chosen from among the elders of the city—Messer Manno Temperani, Messer Carlo Pandolfini,

Messer Giovannozzo Pitti, and Messer Tommaso Soderini. " I will come " was written on certain cards which were hung on the benches covered

Santa Maria Novella.

with arras and placed under the gay pavilion; and the bride did come, and on that platform, made soft with rich carpets, the guests danced and played, waiting for the dinners and suppers. There came to the wedding fifty gentlewomen richly dressed, and fifty gentle youths in beautiful costumes. The gaieties lasted from Sunday morning till Tuesday evening, and there were meals twice a-day. Usually there were asked to each meal fifty persons, including relations, friends and the chief citizens: so that at the first table there were, counting the women and girls of the house, trumpeters and pipers, about one hundred and seventy persons; at the second and third tables — the so-called low tables — there sat a large number of persons. At one meal they amounted to five hundred. The dishes, those prescribed by custom, were exquisite and abundant. On Sunday morning they had boiled capons and tongue, a roast of meat, and another of small chickens garnished with sugar and rosewater; in the evening, galantine, roast-meat and chickens with fritters. Monday morning, *blancmanger*, boiled capons with sausages and roast-chickens; in the evening the usual courses, with tarts of sugar and almonds. On Tuesday morning, roast-meat and quails; in the evening the usual roast and galantine. At the refreshments there appeared twenty confectioners, who distributed a profusion of caramels made of pine-seed. The expenses of these banquets amounted to above 150,000 francs—an immense sum in those day. There had been bought 70 bushels of bread, 2900 white loaves, 4000 wafers, 50 barrels of sweet white wine, 1500 pair of poultry, 1500 eggs, 4 calves, 20 large basins of galantine; 12 *cataste* of wood were burnt in the kitchen-fires. Verily it seemed the reign of abundance. On Tuesday evening some cavaliers invited to the wedding performed

Medici Palace, now Riccardi, end of the 15th century.
(From Politian's edition, 1769).

jousts, moving from the Rucellai Palace up to the Tornaquinci, and afterwards in the Via Larga under the Medici Palace. The bride received from her different relations no fewer than twenty rings, and six more from the bridegroom—two when he fetched her, two for the espousals, and two on the morning they exchanged rings. From Bernardo she received a hundred florins and some other coin, with which she made herself two handsome dresses, one of white velvet richly trimmed with pearls, silk, and gold, with open sleeves lined with pure white fur; one of *zetani*, a stuff of very thick silk, trimmed with pearls, and the sleeves lined with ermine. She had also a gown of white damask brocaded with gold flowers, the sleeves trimmed with pearls; another of silk with crimson, gold, and brocaded sleeves, besides other dresses and overdresses, so-called

Palazzo Riccardi.

giornee. Among the jewels given her was a rich necklet of diamonds, rubies, and pearls, which was worth 100,000 gold florins, a pin for her hair, a necklace of pearls with a large pointed diamond, a hood embroidered with pearls, and a net for her hair, also worked with pearls. The dowry, which to-day would seem modest, was 60,000 francs, including the trousseau, in which was included a pair of chests with richly worked edges and several long dresses of different shapes for everyday wear, made of fine stuffs embroidered, also a lawn shift fashioned out of material that came from Rheims, a hood of crimson cloth wrought with pearls, two caps with silver, pearls, and diamonds, a little illuminated missal with silver clasps, and an infant Jesus in wax wearing a damask dress trimmed with pearls. Besides

The *Duomo* with the façade before 1586.
(From Politian's edition, 1769).

this there was cloth in the piece, satins, velvets, and damasks, embroidered cushions, belts, purses, thimbles, needlecases, ivory combs, four pairs of gloves, a Milanese hat with fringe, eight pairs of stockings, three mirrors, a basin and ewer of enamelled silver, an embroidered fan, and many other things specified in detail.

Giuliano de' Medici and his signet.
(From Politian's edition, 1769).

Three years after, in June 1469, was celebrated with true princely prodigality the marriage of Lorenzo dei Medici and Clarice Orsini, which proved a public feast, a true carnival. "Tu, felix Florentia, nube." We will not stop to describe it, though there is ample information about it to be found in the account which Piero Parenti sent to his maternal uncle, Filippo di Matteo Strozzi, then living at Naples, the founder of the beautiful Strozzi Palace in Florence, that monument to the greatness of the family. These banquets, with their magnificence, embarrassed many of the gentlewomen invited to them, for they were bound to appear in dresses that would

Ponte a Rubaconte now *Ponte alle Grazie*.
(From Politian's edition, 1769).

do honour to the dignity of their families, in robes and gowns of costly brocade and damask. Hence Filippo Strozzi's wife, the lovely and good Fiammetta Adimari, a careful woman, took occasion of her husband's absence to feign illness in order not to be present at the feast. We will follow her example, and search instead in contemporary documents for some signs of intimate domestic life, which grew more rare amid so much public show.

It is pleasant to find this in the little letters which the son of that bride and bridegroom, Piero dei Medici, wrote to his father when away from home, he being left to the care of his pedagogue, Messer Agnolo Poliziano. Much may be forgiven to Piero dei Medici for the sake of these infantine letters, written with the unsteady hand of a five-year-old child, in which appeared his first weak efforts at Latin, which his master did not correct. In 1476, then barely five, he wrote from the Villa to his grandmother, Lucrezia Tornabuoni, with the petulance of an overpetted, spoiled child: " Send us some more figs, I mean those very ripe ones, and send us some peaches with their kernels, and other of those things which you know we like, sweetmeats and tarts and some such little things."

In 1478 he tells his father that he has already learned many verses of Virgil, " and I know the first book of Teodoro by heart, and I think I understand it;" he means Teodoro Gaza's Greek grammar; "and the master makes me decline and examines me every day." The year after, he writes more easily: " I wish you would send me some of the best setters that there are. I don't want anything else. The company here everybody, specially desires to be remembered to you, and so do I. I pray you to be careful of the pestilence and to bear us in mind, because we are little and have need of you." Another time, after a while, he makes use of his Latin to ask for bigger favours. "That little horse has not yet made its appearance" ("Nondum venit equulus ille, magnifice pater"); and he already begins to take a high tone with his younger brothers and sisters. "Guglielmo thinks of nothing else but laughter; Lucrezia sews, sings, and reads; Maddalena knocks her head against the wall without hurting herself; Contessina makes a great noise all over the house." Then he adds, "To give a tone to my letters I have always written them in Latin, and yet I have not had the little horse you promised me, so that everybody laughs at me."

Nevertheless the little horse did not come. "I am afraid something must have happened to the horse, because if it had been all right you would have sent it to me as you promised. If that one cannnot come, please send me another." At last the horse arrived, and a letter full of thanks and promises of good behaviour closes this childish correspondence.

But the curious sketch of Medicean domestic life, which has the country for background, and for stage one of those villas to which they loved to retreat to forget a while political vexations, brings before us another aspect of the time—that desire for country quiet, the love for the villa and the sentiment for nature which are distinguishing characteristics of the men of the Renaissance. We already see signs of this in Ser Lapo Mazzei, who used to go to Grignano to attend the harvests and the vintage and who trimmed his own vines. Buonaccorso Pitti, like Petrarch, loved to count the trees in his garden; Rucellai was prouder of his villa at Quaracchi, of which he gives us a more loving description, than of his splendid palace; Pandolfini, or the compiler of 'The Government of the Family,' sang the praises of country-life; Poliziano wrote a short essay on the theme for his pupils to turn into Latin, and on the background of a flowery landscape he painted the image of the beautiful Simonetta Cattaneo. Lorenzo dei Medici, even in the midst of his greatness as governor, almost prince, knew how to retain a certain benevolent kindness that was quite homely and Florentine; nor did he dislike mingling with the people at the hostelry of the Porta San Gallo. Here he celebrated the beauties of the rustic maiden Nencia, and he ever retained a certain middle-class sobriety. Borghini tells us that Francesco Cibo, at the marriage of his daughter, was treated by Lorenzo with great simplicity and even parsimony, while his companions, Roman cavaliers and barons, were received sumptuously. The Magnifico explained this attitude by saying reassuringly, "These lords I honour as guests and strangers; you, instead, I treat like one of the family." He gave audience to his clients in the streets, by his own fireside, or walking in a friendly manner about the streets of Florence. Florentine to the very core, he did not dislike appearing facetious. At Pisa, seeing a pupil who squinted, he said that he would be the best in the class. Being asked why, he answered, "Because, he will read at once both pages of the book, and so will learn double." Still, under this simple appearance were nurtured the designs of a cunning politician, who, as Vettori writes, "By inducing the citizens to devote themselves to art and pleasure, to the protection of artists of every description, he caused them to become the instruments of his future power."

Under the Medicean rule palaces and convents rose up, in which antiquities, works of art and costly manuscripts were accumulated. In the

Bird's eye view of Florence.
(From Politian's edition, 1769).

gardens artists gathered together, to the supper-parties came poets and philosophers, jousts and tournaments succeeded each other, poetical concourses vied with these feasts, the political clients of the palace were reinforced by the great artists from the humble shops. Savonarola, who guessed the secret thoughts of the tyrant, said, " He occupies the people with tournaments and feasts that they may think of themselves and not of him."

Florence in those times beheld new customs come to life, and listened to many kinds of poetry, from the triumphs and masquerades in the streets to the Platonic banquets at Careggi, from Carnival songs and sweet ballads to country-dances and sacred representations. The thoughtless gaiety, and the ease with which both spiritual and material desires were gratified, seemed to compensate the people for their diminished liberty. The gratified city, which had now for so long resounded with lively, festive clamour, gaily welcomed the great Medicean Carnival with its sumptuous banquets, its processions directed by famous artists and ordered by the brotherhoods of the different quarters. Renascent paganism invaded the religious feasts and transformed these processions for its own end. " In Carnival, " says Cambi, sadly, " the city was made to seem happy and well-to-do. " Folk danced in the New Market, and in the Piazza della Signoria were held shows of wild beasts, when sometimes the lions were let loose in the hope that some terrible scene might take place. But the Florentine lion was so tame, so humble, that it proved as quiet as a lamb. In front of the Medici Palace in Via Larga, *jongleurs* came in crowds to celebrate the triumphs of love. For the arrival of Franceschino Cibo, lately married to Maddalena, daughter of Lorenzo il Magnifico, there were shows in all the shops, pretty and rich things, stuffs and brocade, jewels, pearls, and silver plate, articles of wonderful and surprising beauty. On St John's Day was performed a beautiful spectacle of clouds and spirits,

Palazzo della Signoria, end of the 15th century.
(From Politian's edition, 1769).

cars and other fairy edifices, popular contrivances to pass the time, besides all the other gaieties of the season. Magnificent races were held; the tower of the Palazzo Vecchio was red amid the crackling of the fireworks. On the occasion of the coming of orators or at the creation of knights, the noble Signoria was wont to hold solemn ceremonies, of which we find record in the book of Francesco Filarete, herald to the Republic. In 1491, on St John's Day, Lorenzo had set up fifteen erections representing the triumph of

Paolo Emilio after his return from Macedonia, when he bore with him so much treasure that for many years the Romans were free from taxes. It seemed as though the golden age had come back. The Medicean jousts which had inspired Poliziano's muse stimulated the other citizens to commit mad extravagances. Benedetto Salutati, nephew of Messer Coluccio, for the tournament of 1467 put on the housings, head-gear, and other trappings of two horses one hundred and seventy pounds of fine silver, which he caused to be beautifully worked by the hand of Antonio Pollajolo; and around the robes of the sergeants he strung thirty pounds of pearls, the greater part of which were of immense value. Florence beautified itself with splendid palaces; Filippo Strozzi, on the 6th of August 1489, laid the foundation of his stately pile, and Guglielmo Gondi, a short time after, followed his example. The people were proud of these new buildings, and good Tribaldo dei Rossi asked his wife Nannina to send him his two chidren, newly dressed, that he might take them to see the laying of the cornerstone of the Strozzi Palace. "I took," he writes, "Guarnieri in my arms, and told him to look down there. I gave him a coin with a lily to throw down, also a bunch of little damask roses which I had in my hand. I said, 'Will you remember this?' He said, 'Yes.' The children came with our servant Rita, and Guarnieri, who was on that day just four years old, had a new cloak made by Nannina of shot green-and-yellow silk." The children as well as the older citizens must have been struck by the surprising marvels which the Medicean magnificence displayed for their benefit. Every day some new and singular thing occurred—princely jousts and processions, magnificent feasts. De Rossi, a simple chronicler, has kept for us a record of these events. In 1488 there came to Florence, as a present from the Sultan of Babylonia to Lorenzo, a giraffe, which was seven *braccias* high, led by two Turks. Great curiosity was awakened in every one, even in the nuns, so that it was needful to send the strange beast around to the convents to be inspected. " It eats everything, poking its

The *giraffe*.
(From a miniature by Attavante, at Venice).

head into every peasant's basket, and would take an apple from a child's hand, so gentle is it. It died on the 2^d of January 1489, and everybody lamented it, for it was such a beautiful animal."

The portrait of Savonarola.

Suddenly, quite suddenly, this easy mirthful life, this dazzling splendour of art and poetry, this thoughtless gaiety, was extinguished sadly and gloomily. A tempest murmured in the distance. The proud Dominican shut up in his monastery of San Marco, far from the uproar of the Carnival, threatened resuscitated paganism with celestial anger. On the 8th of April 1492 there fell like a public calamity the news that Lorenzo dei Medici was dead. "The splendour, not of Tuscany only, but of the whole of Italy, has disappeared," writes Dei. "The company of the Magi laid the body in the sacristy of San Lorenzo, and the day after the funeral services took place without pomp, as is the custom for nobles, but simply, devoid of hangings and canopies, with three

The cloisters of St. Mark.

orders of friars and only one of priests. For no matter how pompous the ceremony might have been, it would always have proved too mean for so great a man."

Thus with lugubrious obsequies in the chill twilight of the Laurentian sepulchre, with the remains of the Magnifico were laid to rest the memories of a whole age radiant with youth and glory. With Lorenzo there disappeared the world of the Renaissance, for but a little time afterwards Tribaldo de Rossi writes: "A letter has come to the Signoria saying that certain youths, gone out in sailing-ships, have arrived at an immense island, to which never before have any people sailed, which is inhabited by men and women all naked."

A new world had been discovered.

The cell of Savonarola.

LIST OF ILLUSTRATIONS

The Marzocco............................Page	5
Or San Michele. Shrine by Orcagna...............	6
Santa Reparata and the Campanile. (From a Laurentian Ms.)..	7
The Baptistery. (Miniature in the Biadajolo, a Laurentian Ms.).	8
The Cornchandler. (Miniature in the Biadajolo).........	9
Santa Reparata and the Campanile. (Miniature in the Biadajolo).	10
Loggia del Bigallo by Orcagna...................	11
A plan of Florence. (Chronicles of Nüremberg).........	12
Or San Michele, with the old shrine. (Miniature in the Biadajolo).	17
A view of the demolished Ancient Market............	18
The Devil by Giambologna.....................	19
Painting by Domenico di Michelino in the Duomo. (From an old engraving in the Laurentian Library)..............	25
Fresco in the Monastery of Lecceto near Siena..........	33
The prisons Le Stinche. (From an engraving in Politian's Conjurationis Pactianae Commentarium, edited by I. Adimari, 1769).	60
The Canto dei Pazzi, at the corner of Borgo degli Albizi. (From Politian's edition, 1769)...................	62
Consecration of the Duomo by Pope Eugenius 4th. (From a Missal in the Laurentian Library)................	63
The Duomo, end of the 15th century. (From a Laurentian miniature).	64
The Palace of the Podestà, end of the 15th century. (From Politian's edition, 1769).....................	66
Santa Maria Novella........................	72
Medici Palace, now Riccardi, end of the 15th century. (From Politian's edition, 1769).....................	74
Palazzo Riccardi..........................	75

The *Duomo* with the façade before 1586. (From Politian's edition, 1769) . . . . Page 76
Giuliano de' Medici and his signet. (From Politian's edition, 1769). 77
Ponte a Rubaconte now *Ponte alle Grazie*. (From Politian's edition, 1769) 78
Bird's eye view of Florence. (From Politian's edition, 1769) . . 83
Palazzo della Signoria, end of the 15th century. (From Politian's edition, 1769) 85
The *giraffe*. (From a miniature by Attavante, at Venice) 87
The portrait of Savonarola 88
The cloisters of St. Mark 89
The cell of Savonarola 90

www.ingramcontent.com/pod-product-compliance
Lightning Source LLC
Chambersburg PA
CBHW020302090426
42735CB00009B/1192